Inside the NFL

THE
BUFFALO
BILLS

BOB ITALIA
ABDO & Daughters

Published by Abdo & Daughters, 4940 Viking Drive, Suite 622, Edina, Minnesota 55435.

Printed in the United States.

Cover Photo credits: Wide World Photos/Allsport
Interior Photo credits: Wide World Photos

Edited by Kal Gronvall

Library of Congress Cataloging-in-Publication Data

Italia, Bob, 1955- The Buffalo Bills / Bob Italia.
    p. cm. — (Inside the NFL)
Includes index.
Summary: Presents a history of the National League football team that has been in four straight Super Bowls without winning.
ISBN 1-56239-525-4
1. Buffalo Bills (football team)—Juvenile literature. [1. Buffalo Bills, (Football team). I. Title. II. Series: Italia, Bob, 1955- Inside the NFL.
GV956.B83I83 1995
796.332'f,4'09747'37—dc20   95-19503
                                                     CIP
                                                     AC

CONTENTS

The Buffalo Dynasty

The Buffalo Bills are the only National Football League (NFL) team that can lay claim to a football dynasty without having won a single Super Bowl. From 1990 to 1993, Buffalo won a record-four consecutive AFC championships. Their four-straight Super Bowl appearances is also an NFL record. It may be a long time before such a team makes another run at championship history.

Head coach Marv Levy helped build the Buffalo football dynasty.

A football dynasty is not built without great players. Throughout their history, the Bills have had their share of offensive and defensive stars. In the early years, there was Jack Kemp, Daryle Lamonica, Pete Gogolak, Cookie Gilchrist, O.J. Simpson, and Joe Ferguson. In the championship years, Jim Kelly, Thurman Thomas, Andre Reed, Cornelius Bennett, and Bruce Smith led the way.

The Bills will always be remembered as the first NFL team to lose four straight Super Bowls. But Bills fans can take heart in knowing that—for seven consecutive years—Buffalo ruled the American Football Conference.

Opposite page: Running back Thurman Thomas led the Bills to four-straight Super Bowls.

An AFL Beginning

In 1950, Buffalo, New York, lost its professional football team when the All-America Football Conference joined the National Football League (NFL). Buffalo citizens enjoyed professional sports. It wanted an NFL team. The league, however, did not cooperate.

But then Lamar Hunt stepped into the picture. Hunt was a wealthy Texas businessman who made his fortune selling Hunt's Catsup. He asked the NFL for a franchise. The NFL turned him down.

Hunt refused to quit. He and some business associates formed a new football league— the American Football League (AFL). One of Hunt's partners was Ralph C. Wilson. He wanted his own team. Hunt suggested Buffalo. In 1959, Wilson contacted the city leaders and leased Buffalo's War Memorial Stadium. Wilson named his team the Bills—in honor of Western hero Buffalo Bill Cody. The Bills named Garrard Ramsey as the head coach. But the Bills did not have a winning season in 1960 or 1961.

Buffalo's War Memorial Stadium.

Lou Saban

Lou Saban replaced Ramsey in 1962. Saban had been a quarterback at Indiana University in the early 1940s. He could turn talented players into winners. Among those early stars were wide receiver Elbert Dubenion, fullback Cookie Gilchrist, kicker Pete Gogolak, and quarterbacks Jack Kemp, Daryle Lamonica, and Warren Rabb.

Rabb became famous for his last minute heroics. On October 28, 1962, with 11:57 left to play, Buffalo trailed Denver 38-23. Rabb tossed a 75-yard touchdown pass, a 40-yard touchdown pass, made a two-point conversion, then ran in another touchdown—all in the last quarter. Rabb's heroics gave Buffalo a 45-38 win over Denver.

Dubenion was the Bills' first big star. He could read defenses, make the big catch, and run for additional yardage. His skills earned him the nickname "Golden Wheels." It also earned him Bills' pass reception records that still stand today.

Gilchrist came to Buffalo in 1962 from the Canadian Football League (CFL). He immediately became a star. Gilchrist was the first AFL back to gain over 1,000 yards in a season. Since he was so big, Gilchrist was difficult to bring down. In a game against the New York Jets, Gilchrist scored five touchdowns and rushed for 243 yards, helping Buffalo rout New York 45-14.

Gogolak signed in 1964 from Cornell University. He brought soccer-style kicking to the AFL. At first, fans laughed at his strange kicking style. But Gogolak booted 47 field goals in his two years with the team.

Head coach Lou Saban helped build
the Bills into AFL champions.

AFL Champions

From 1962 to 1966, Jack Kemp and Daryle Lamonica led the Bills to five-straight winning seasons and two consecutive AFL championships (1964 and 1965). The Kemp/Lamonica duo worked well. They formed one of the league's most potent offensive machines.

Kemp was a 1957 graduate of Occidental College. He came to Buffalo in mid-1962 from the San Diego Chargers. Although he only appeared in four games that year, Kemp made the All-Star game. He also led Buffalo to a winning season after an 0-5 start.

Lamonica was known as the "Mad Bomber" because he threw long touchdown passes. In the 1963 playoff game against Boston, Lamonica threw a 93-yard touchdown strike in a 26-8 loss. In 1967, he was traded to the Oakland Raiders.

In 1966, Saban left the team for the University of Maryland. Assistant coach Joe Collier became head coach. Lamonica and Gilchrist were traded, and the championship team had weakened.

Quarterback Jack Kemp (15) celebrates a championship with his teammates.

O.J. Simpson

The Bills finished last in 1967 and 1968. This gave Buffalo the first round selection in the 1969 college draft. The Bills' pick, Heisman Trophy winner Orenthal James "O. J." Simpson, would become one of football's greatest stars.

While a senior at the University of Southern California (USC), Simpson broke NCAA records for carries and rushing yards. Simpson won the Heisman voting by the largest point margin ever.

Simpson had a hard life as a child. He grew up in a San Francisco ghetto. There, he suffered from rickets, a crippling bone disease. His doctors had to give him leg braces. They told him he could never play football. But Simpson did not give up his dream of one day playing professional football.

As he grew older, Simpson's path to pro football got sidetracked. He got involved with street gangs and spent time in jail. But eventually, sports became his salvation.

Simpson starred for the Galileo High School team as a senior. But low grades and the school's poor football program kept Simpson out of a major college.

Simpson enrolled in the two-year City College of San Francisco. There, he broke many national junior college rushing and scoring records. His accomplishments gained him the attention of major college coaches from around the nation.

Simpson eventually chose USC because he had watched their football team on television as a teenager. In addition to playing football, Simpson was also part of the world record-setting USC 440-yard relay team.

Simpson's early years at Buffalo were frustrating. Coach Jim Rauch did not want to build his offense around a running back.

Simpson was losing his edge on the playing field. In 1969 and 1970, he ran for less than 700 yards. Buffalo struggled through two more losing seasons. Simpson thought of quitting the team.

But then Rauch and owner Ralph Wilson got into a quarrel. Rauch resigned before the start of the 1971 season. Scout Harvey Johnson stepped in. But the Bills finished with a 1-13-0 record

Lou Saban returned to coach the Bills in 1972. His arrival gave Simpson and his teammates new life. They knew Saban favored the running game.

Simpson won the league rushing title in 1972 with 1,251 yards. Though the team only finished at 4-9-1, Buffalo was a team on the rise.

Much of the credit went to coach Saban's creation of "The Electric Company." They were an offensive unit designed to turn on "The Juice," as Simpson was known.

Through trades and the college draft, Saban collected a strong offensive team. Joe DeLamielleure, Reggie McKenzie, Joe Ferguson, Dave Foley, Mike Montler, Jeff Winans and J. D. Hill were among the many stars.

In the December 16, 1973, season-ending matchup at home against the New York Jets, Simpson set his eyes on the record books. Going into the game, Simpson had 1,803 yards rushing—only 60 yards short of Jim Brown's season rushing record.

The field was cold and icy. But Simpson's blockers punched holes in the Jets' defense. By the fourth quarter, Simpson had broken Brown's record. For the season, he finished with 2,003 yards—a record that stood until 1984, when Eric Dickerson of the Los Angeles Rams rushed for 2, 105 yards.

Simpson and his offensive line gave the Bills two more winning seasons in 1974 and 1975. But Simpson was unhappy. The 1976 season ended with a frustrating 2-12 record. Saban left the team once again. Stars such as Ahmad Rashad, Pat Toomey, and J. D. Hill were traded. Then, in the October 30, 1977, game against Seattle, Simpson injured his knee. He asked to be traded.

Chuck Knox

In March 1978, the Bills' new head coach Chuck Knox traded Simpson to the San Francisco 49ers for five future draft choices. In two years, Knox created a strong defensive team. Knox already had a strong offense. Quarterback Joe Ferguson had become a star.

A Louisiana native, Ferguson played for the University of Arkansas Razorbacks. While at Arkansas, Ferguson perfected the long passes that made him the Bills' leading passer from 1973 to 1984. He was voted an All-American during his junior year.

Head coach Chuck Knox shouts instructions to his team.

The Buffalo offense also had a young running back who came to the Bills as part of the O. J. Simpson trade. A number-two draft pick from the University of Auburn, Joe Cribbs led Buffalo in rushing for four straight seasons, and finished second only to O. J. Simpson in total rushing yards with Buffalo.

Buffalo's defense also had its stars. There was Fred Smerlas and Jim Haslett, standouts at Boston College and Indiana University of Pennsylvania. Linebackers Isiah Robertson and Phil Vilipiano were obtained in trades with the Los Angeles Rams and the Oakland Raiders.

The Bills appeared in AFC divisional playoffs in 1980 and 1981. Though they did not reach the Super Bowl, the Bills seemed only a few steps away.

In 1982, the players strike disrupted Knox's rebuilding plans. Then he lost star running back Joe Cribbs over a salary dispute. Discouraged, Knox left for a new job in Seattle.

Assistant coach Kay Stephenson took over as head coach. Stephenson guided Buffalo to an 8-8 record in 1983. But then the Bills finished 2-14 in 1984 and 1985 and 4-12 in 1986. Midway through the 1985 season, Hank Bullough replaced Stephenson. But Bullough had little success.

Knox and lineman Reggie McKenzie celebrate a victory.

13

The Levy Era

Marv Levy became Bills' head coach during the 1986 season. Levy had college and professional coaching experience that helped energize Buffalo. In 1987, Levy led the team to a 7-8 record. In 1988 and 1989, the Bills won the AFC's Eastern Division.

Head coach Marv Levy.

Levy had many talented young players to thank. Defensive end Bruce Smith, an All-American from Virginia Tech, was among the league's most feared pass rushers. He and linebackers Cornelius Bennett and Shane Conlan were perennial All-Pros.

Leading the offense was Buffalo's star quarterback, Jim Kelly. Kelly came to the Bills in 1986 after two seasons with the United States Football League's (USFL's) Houston Gamblers. Kelly led the University of Miami Hurricanes to the Peach Bowl in 1980.

In 1988, the Bills' defense was the best in the AFC. Bennett and Conlan made the Pro Bowl. Nose tackle Fred Smerlas had one of his best seasons. Kelly and rookie running back Thurman Thomas also played well. Though the Bills slumped toward the end of the season, their 12-4 record clinched the Eastern Division title.

In the first round of the playoffs, the Bills defeated the Houston Oilers 17-10. But in the AFC championship game, they lost to the Cincinnati Bengals 21-10. Despite the setback, the Bills seemed ready to take the next step to the Super Bowl.

In 1989, the Bills were the NFL's second-highest scoring team, averaging 27 points per game. Kelly was the AFC's top-rated passer. Wide receiver Andre Reed was the AFC's leading receiver. Running back Thurman Thomas led the NFL in rushing.

But Buffalo had more than its share of injuries. Conlan, Bennett and Kelly missed games. Buffalo finished with a 9-7 record—good enough to repeat as division champions for the first time since the 1960s. But injuries hurt them in the first playoff round as they lost 34-30 to the Cleveland Browns.

Defensive lineman Bruce Smith leads the charge against Miami in the playoffs.

The Super Bowl Legacy Begins

Buffalo entered the 1990 season with a healthy team and a winning attitude. They quickly established themselves as the AFC's most complete team. Smith, Bennett, Conlan, and Darryl Talley anchored a rock-solid defense. Kelly, Thomas, and Reed led the AFC's best offense. Buffalo won the Eastern title for the third straight year with a 13-3 record. This time, they were determined to go all the way.

In their first playoff game, Buffalo overwhelmed Miami 44-34. The Bills jumped out to a 27-17 halftime lead and never looked back. In the AFC championship game against the Raiders, the Bills were nearly perfect as they destroyed Los Angeles 51-3. Their 48-point margin of victory was the second largest ever—behind only the Chicago Bears' 73-0 beating of the Washington Redskins in 1940.

Buffalo stormed out to a 21-3 lead at the end of the first quarter. By halftime it was 41-3. All of Buffalo's second quarter scores were drives of more than 50 yards. The Bills stayed on the ground in the second half, but still tacked on another 10 points. Buffalo was now going to the Super Bowl for the first time to face the New York Giants.

The Bills were favored by a touchdown to win the championship. They took a 12-10 halftime lead but fell behind in the third quarter 17-12. With 1:19 left in that quarter, the Bills started a drive from their 37 that ended in Thomas' 31-yard touchdown run on the first play of the fourth quarter.

Thurman Thomas breaks free from the Giants' defense.

Down 19-17, the Giants put together another long scoring drive and took the lead 20-19 with a field goal. But Buffalo wasn't finished.

In the final two minutes, the Bills drove from their own 10 to the New York 29. But Scott Norwood's attempt for a 47-yard, game-winning field goal sailed wide right.

**Opposite page:
Scott Norwood's
Super Bowl-winning
field goal attempt.**

Buffalo Bills

Lou Saban joins the team in 1962.

O.J. Simpson rushes for a record 2,003 yards in 1973.

Jack Kemp leads the Bills to consecutive AFL championships in 1964 and 1965.

20   30   40

10   20   30   40

40   20   10

Bruce Smith signs with the Bills in 1985.

In 1993, Buffalo plays in its record-fourth-straight Super Bowl.

Buffalo Bills

Jim Kelly leaves the USFL to join the Bills in 1986.

40   30   20   10

Getting Better

The 1990 Super Bowl loss was a defeat most teams could not rebound from. But the Bills were hardly an ordinary team. In 1991, Buffalo won 10 of its first 11 games behind a no-huddle offense that dominated the NFL. Jim Kelly led the league with 33 touchdown passes, and Thomas was named the league's most valuable player. He rushed for 1,407 yards, caught 61 passes for 631 yards and scored 12 touchdowns. Reed led all receivers with 81 catches and 10 touchdowns.

But there were chinks in the armor. Smith missed most of the season with a knee injury, and the team finished 27th in the NFL in yards allowed. Still, Buffalo finished with a 13-3 record for their fourth consecutive Eastern title.

In the playoffs, Buffalo had little problem with Kansas City as they defeated the Chiefs 37-14. Their biggest challenge would come against John Elway and the Denver Broncos in the AFC championship game.

Denver held the high-powered Bills without an offensive touchdown. But the Broncos offense was stifled by the Bills' defense.

Unheralded linebacker Carlton Bailey emerged as the hero with an 11-yard interception return for a touchdown that gave the Bills a 7-0 lead in the third quarter. Scott Norwood added to the lead in the fourth quarter with a 44-yard field goal. But Denver scored a touchdown with 1:28 to play.

Still, victory seemed certain—until the Broncos recovered an onside kick. Denver had a chance to tie the game, but they fumbled away their chances with seconds to play. The Bills were going to their second straight Super Bowl.

In 1991, Jim Kelly led the league in touchdown passes.

Kelly is sacked in Super Bowl XXVI.

In Super Bowl XXVI against the Redskins, Buffalo and Washington played to a 0-0 first quarter. Then the bottom dropped out. The Redskins scored 17 second quarter points for a 17-0 halftime lead.

In the third quarter, Washington added another touchdown for a 24-0 lead before Buffalo responded with a 21-yard Norwood field goal and a 1-yard Thomas touchdown run to make the score 24-10. Another third quarter Redskins touchdown killed any hopes of a Buffalo comeback. The Bills' 37-24 loss was their second straight Super Bowl defeat.

Wild Card Champions

The Bills failed to win the AFC East crown in 1992. But it was still a successful season as they finished 11-5. The defense improved, and Thomas led the league in total yards for the fourth straight year, breaking Jim Brown's record. Kelly had a good season, but led the league in interceptions thrown with 19. Few experts thought the Bills would return to the Super Bowl.

In the first round of the playoffs, Buffalo faced the Houston Oilers without Jim Kelly, who was injured. Led by quarterback Warren Moon, Houston had a high-powered offense. They exploded for 21 second-quarter points and took a seemingly insurmountable 28-3 halftime lead. To make matters worse, Houston added to their lead in the third quarter on a 58-yard interception return for a touchdown. Buffalo's long playoff run seemed ready to end.

But then a miracle happened. Kelly's replacement, Frank Reich, suddenly found his rhythm. He led Buffalo to four third-quarter touchdowns—including three touchdown passes. Reich's passing frenzy brought the Bills to within 35-31.

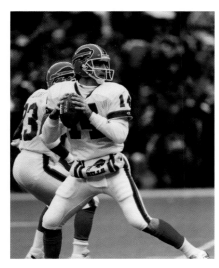

In the 1992 playoffs, Frank Reich played well for the injured Jim Kelly.

Buffalo took the lead 38-35 in the fourth quarter on another Reich touchdown pass. But Houston managed to rally for a game-tying field goal that sent the game into overtime. Reich directed another drive that set up newcomer Steve Christie's game-winning 32-yard field goal. It was a miraculous win. But to get to the Super Bowl, Buffalo would have to win two more road games. Experts still did not give them much of a chance.

In the second playoff round, Buffalo had an easy time with Pittsburgh. Reich started in place of Kelly and threw two touchdown passes for a 24-3 win. It was another impressive victory. But now the Bills would have to face Dan Marino and the Dolphins in Miami for the AFC championship. No one expected them to win.

But the Bills surprised everyone with a convincing 29-10 victory. Smith played a great game, with seven tackles, one and a half sacks, a forced fumble, and a blocked pass. Thomas rushed for 96 yards and caught five passes for 70 yards. Christie tied a playoff record with five field goals. And Kelly returned to the lineup to throw for 177 yards and one touchdown.

But the defense was the real star. Marino could not dent the Buffalo defense. They sacked him four times and flustered him the entire game.

With the victory, Buffalo qualified for a record-tying third straight Super Bowl. They became the fourth wildcard team to make it to the Super Bowl.

The Bills seemed ready to break the Super Bowl jinx. They had won three improbable victories and appeared ready for the heavily favored Dallas Cowboys.

Super Bowl XXVII had the markings of a truly great game until just before halftime. That's when Buffalo became unglued and Dallas turned an uneasy 14-10 lead into a 28-10 rout that continued throughout the second half.

The Bills lost the ball nine times—five fumbles and four interceptions—and they led directly to five Dallas touchdowns. The most costly turnover was a Jim Kelly interception on a fourth-down play at the Dallas one-yard line early in the second quarter. Shortly after, Kelly was injured and sat out the rest of the game. Dallas' margin of victory was the third-largest in a Super Bowl. Buffalo's third-straight Super Bowl loss was another record.

Four-in-a-Row

It seemed improbable that the Bills could continue their domination of the AFC after their Super Bowl loss. But dominate—and improve—they did in 1993. Smith was the NFL's Defensive Player of the Year and tied for the league lead with 13.5 sacks. Kelly passed for 3,382 yards and 18 touchdowns, and Thomas led the AFC with 1,315 yards rushing. The Bills won the Eastern division again with a 12-4 record—and set their sights on a record-fourth straight AFC title.

In the divisional playoffs, Buffalo got into a dog fight with the Raiders. At halftime, they trailed 17-13. By the end of the third quarter, the Bills trailed 23-22. But a 22-yard touchdown pass from Kelly to Bill Brooks saved the day for Buffalo as the Bills won 29-23. Now they would play Joe Montana and the Kansas City Chiefs in Buffalo.

In the game, Thomas almost single-handedly led the Bills to a 30-10 victory. Thomas carried the ball 33 times for 186 yards and three touchdowns as the Bills earned their record-setting fourth consecutive Super Bowl trip.

Andre Reed streaks for the goal line against the Chiefs in the AFC championship game.

In Super Bowl XXVII against the Cowboys, it seemed the Bills would finally get that elusive victory. In the first half, they played

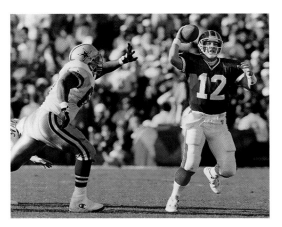

A Dallas defender pressures Jim Kelly.

tough defense and held the high-powered Dallas offense to only six points. Meanwhile, a 4-yard Thomas touchdown run and three Christie field goals put the Bills ahead 13-6 at halftime. But Dallas ruled the second half, shutting out the Bills while racking up 24 points for a 30-13 win.

Thomas had another poor Super Bowl. He gained only 37 yards on 16 carries and fumbled twice. Kelly put the ball into the air 50 times, completing 31 passes. But he could not find the end zone.

§

The Bills amazing playoff streak finally came to an end in 1994 as they failed to make the playoffs for the first time since 1987. Kelly, Smith, and Thomas still made up the core of the team, but they were getting older. Perhaps, after four Super Bowl losses, the competitive fire was dwindling. Perhaps the Bills were finally on the decline. The coming years would tell whether the Bills could recapture their lost glory—or be forced to rebuild. Whatever the outcome, the Buffalo dynasty remains one of the most remarkable stories in NFL history.

GLOSSARY

ALL-PRO—A player who is voted to the Pro Bowl.

BACKFIELD—Players whose position is behind the line of scrimmage.

CORNERBACK—Either of two defensive halfbacks stationed a short distance behind the linebackers and relatively near the sidelines.

DEFENSIVE END—A defensive player who plays on the end of the line and often next to the defensive tackle.

DEFENSIVE TACKLE—A defensive player who plays on the line and between the guard and end.

ELIGIBLE—A player who is qualified to be voted into the Hall of Fame.

END ZONE—The area on either end of a football field where players score touchdowns.

EXTRA POINT—The additional one-point score added after a player makes a touchdown. Teams earn extra points if the placekicker kicks the ball through the uprights of the goalpost, or if an offensive player crosses the goal line with the football before being tackled.

FIELD GOAL—A three-point score awarded when a placekicker kicks the ball through the uprights of the goalpost.

FULLBACK—An offensive player who often lines up farthest behind the front line.

FUMBLE—When a player loses control of the football.

GUARD—An offensive lineman who plays between the tackles and center.

GROUND GAME—The running game.

HALFBACK—An offensive player whose position is behind the line of scrimmage.

HALFTIME—The time period between the second and third quarters of a football game.

INTERCEPTION—When a defensive player catches a pass from an offensive player.

KICK RETURNER—An offensive player who returns kickoffs.

LINEBACKER—A defensive player whose position is behind the line of scrimmage.

LINEMAN—An offensive or defensive player who plays on the line of scrimmage.

PASS—To throw the ball.

PASS RECEIVER—An offensive player who runs pass routes and catches passes.

PLACEKICKER—An offensive player who kicks extra points and field goals. The placekicker also kicks the ball from a tee to the opponent after his team has scored.

PLAYOFFS—The postseason games played amongst the division winners and wild card teams which determines the Super Bowl champion.

PRO BOWL—The postseason All-Star game which showcases the NFL's best players.

PUNT—To kick the ball to the opponent.

QUARTER—One of four 15-minute time periods that makes up a football game.

QUARTERBACK—The backfield player who usually calls the signals for the plays.

REGULAR SEASON—The games played after the preseason and before the playoffs.

ROOKIE—A first-year player.

RUNNING BACK—A backfield player who usually runs with the ball.

RUSH—To run with the football.

SACK—To tackle the quarterback behind the line of scrimmage.

SAFETY—A defensive back who plays behind the linemen and linebackers. Also, two points awarded for tackling an offensive player in his own end zone when he's carrying the ball.

SPECIAL TEAMS—Squads of football players that perform special tasks (for example, kickoff team and punt-return team).

SPONSOR—A person or company that finances a football team.

SUPER BOWL—The NFL championship game played between the AFC champion and the NFC champion.

T FORMATION—An offensive formation in which the fullback lines up behind the center and quarterback with one halfback stationed on each side of the fullback.

TACKLE—An offensive or defensive lineman who plays between the ends and the guards.

TAILBACK—The offensive back farthest from the line of scrimmage.

TIGHT END—An offensive lineman who is stationed next to the tackles, and who usually blocks or catches passes.

TOUCHDOWN—When one team crosses the goal line of the other team's end zone. A touchdown is worth six points.

TURNOVER—To turn the ball over to an opponent either by a fumble, an interception, or on downs.

UNDERDOG—The team that is picked to lose the game.

WIDE RECEIVER—An offensive player who is stationed relatively close to the sidelines and who usually catches passes.

WILD CARD—A team that makes the playoffs without winning its division.

ZONE PASS DEFENSE—A pass defense method where defensive backs defend a certain area of the playing field rather than individual pass receivers.

INDEX